Series: Fun with Arabic Writing Part II

Shape and Forms of Arabic Letters

A Coloring and Activity Book

Level: Pre-School / Elementary

Assad Nimer Busool

IQRA INTERNATIONAL EDUCATIONAL FOUNDATION
Chicago

Ḍâd

Ḍifdi‘	**Frog**
Qaḍîb	**Staff**
Baiḍ	**Eggs**

Ṭâ

Ṭair	**Bird**
Qiṭar	**Train**
Khaiṭ	**Thread**

Ẓâ

Ẓufr	**Nail**
Naẓẓârah	**Glasses**
Wâ‘iẓ	**Preacher**

‘Ain

‘Inab	**Grapes**
Sha‘r	**Hair**
Jāmi‘	**Mosque**

Ghain

Ghurâb	**Crow**
Baghl	**Mule**
Ṣamgh	**Glue**

Fâ

Famm	**Mouth**
Qafaṣ	**Cage**
’Anf	**Nose**

Qâf

Qur’ân	**Qur’ân**
‘Iqd	**Necklace**
Ibrîq	**Pitcher**

Kâf

Ka‘bah	**Ka‘bah**
Maktab	**Desk**
Malik	**King**

Lâm

Lift	**Turnip**
Qalam	**Pen**
Ḥabl	**Rope**

Mîm

Mishṭ	**Comb**
Sham‘ah	**Candle**
‘Alam	**Flag**

Nûn

Naḥlah	**Bee**
Manârah	**Minaret**
‘Ain	**Eye**

Hâ

Hilâl	**Crescent**
Nahr	**River**
Furshah	**Brush**

Wâw

Walad	**Boy**
Ṣûf	**Wool**
Dalw	**Bucket**

Yâ

Yad	**Hand**
Ṭayyârah	**Aeroplane**
Kursî	**Chair**

GLOSSARY

Alif

Arnab	**Rabbit**
Sâʻah	**Watch**
Kûsa	**Zucchini**

Bâ

Baqarah	**Cow**
Jabal	**Mountain**
ʻInab	**Grapes**

Tâ

Tuffâḥ	**Apples**
Kitâb	**Book**
Takht	**Bed**

Thâ

Thaʻlab	**Fox**
Muthallath	**Triangle**
Laith	**Lion**

Jîm

Jamal	**Camel**
Shajarah	**Tree**
Thalj	**Ice/Snow**

Ḥâ

Ḥiṣân	**Horse**
Ṣaḥn	**Plate**
Rumḥ	**Lance**

Khâ

Kharûf	**Lamb**
Nakhlah	**Date tree**
Baṭṭîkh	**Watermelon**

Dâl

Dîk	**Rooster**
Hud Hud	**Hoopoe**
ʻIqd	**Necklace**

Dhâl

Dhurah	**Corn**
Ḥidhâ'	**Shoe**
Juradh	**Rat**

Râ

Rajul	**Man**
Burtuqāl	**Orange(s)**
Qamar	**Moon**

Zâ

Zahrah	**Flower**
Mîzân	**Balance, Scale**
ʻAnz	**Goat**

Sîn

Samak	**Fish(s)**
Lisân	**Tongue**
Libs	**Dress**

Shîn

Shams	**Sun**
Minshâr	**Saw**
Rafsh	**Spade**

Ṣâd

Ṣûṣ	**Chick**
Baṣal	**Onion**
Miqaṣṣ	**Scissors**

Yā

ي ياء ي

Yad 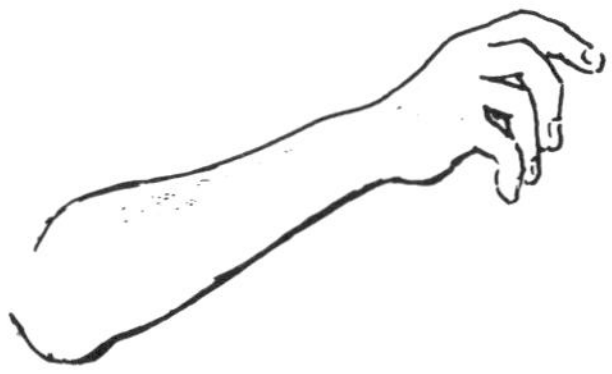 يَد

Ṭayyārah 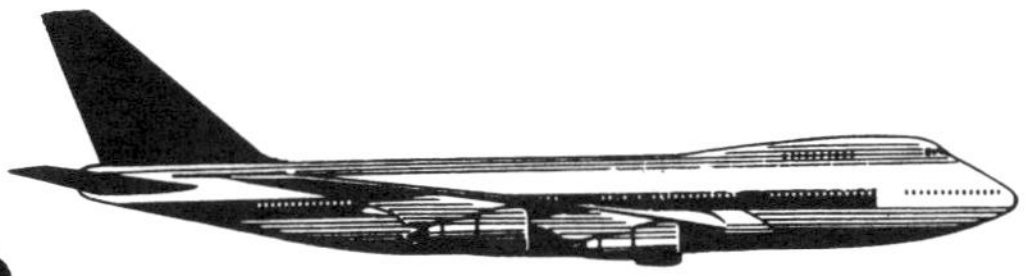 طَيَّارَة

Kursī  كُرْسِيّ

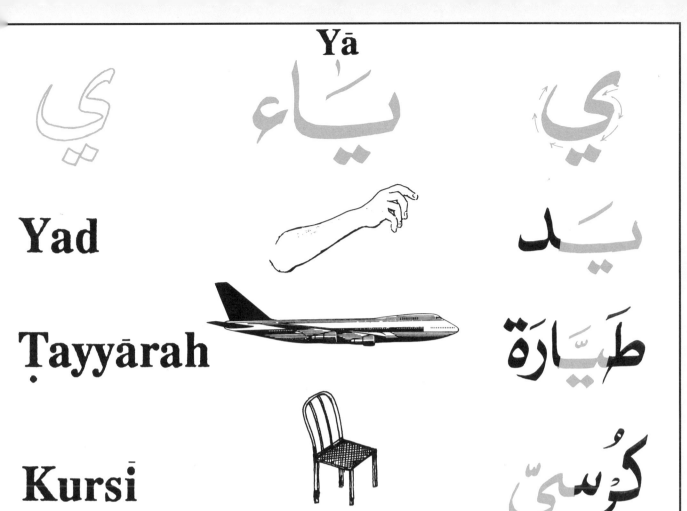

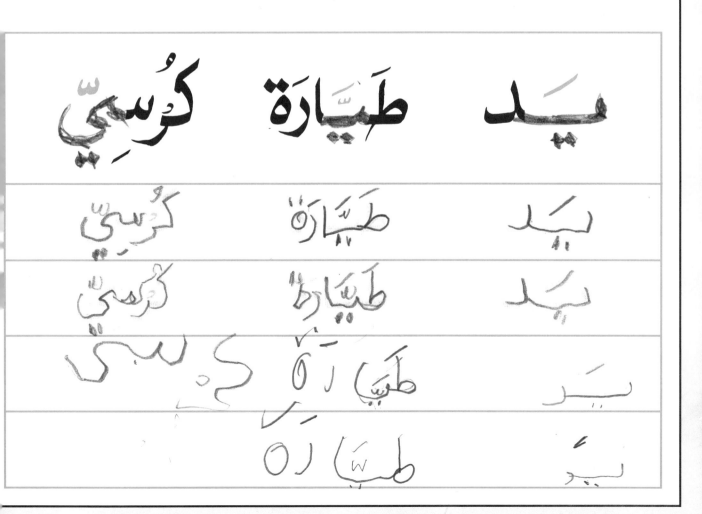

يَد طَيَّارَة كُرْسِيّ

Wāw

و واو و

Walad  وَلَد

Ṣūf  صُوف

Dalw  دَلُو

وَلَد صُوف دَلُو

وَلَد صُوف دَلُو

وَلَد صُوف دَلُو

Hā

هـ هـاء هـ

Hilāl  هِلَال

Nahr  نَهْر

Furshah  فُرْشَة

هِلَال نَهْر فُرْشَة

هلال نهر فرشة

هلال نهر فرشة

Nūn

ن نون ن

Nahlah  نحلة

Manārah  منارة

'Ain  عين

نحلة منارة عين

Mīm

م ميم م

مِشْط  **Misht**

شَمْعَة  **Sham‘ah**

عَلَم  **‘Alam**

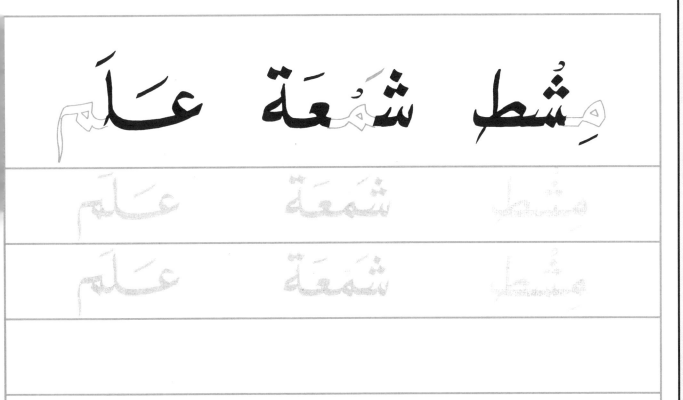

مِشْط شَمْعَة عَلَم

مشط شمعة علم

مشط شمعة علم

Lām

ل لام ل

Lift  لِفُت

Qalam  قَلَم

Ḥabl  حَبُل

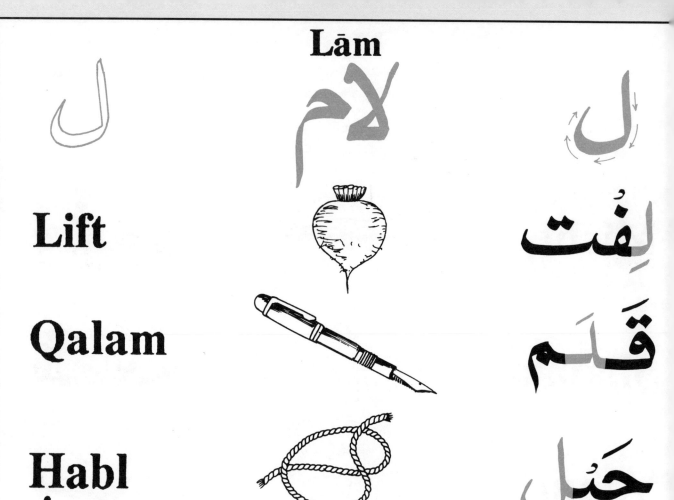

لِفُت قَلَم حَبُل

لِفُت قَلَم حَبُل

لِفُت قَلَم حَبُل

Kāf

ك كاف ك

Ka'bah  كَعْبَة

Maktab 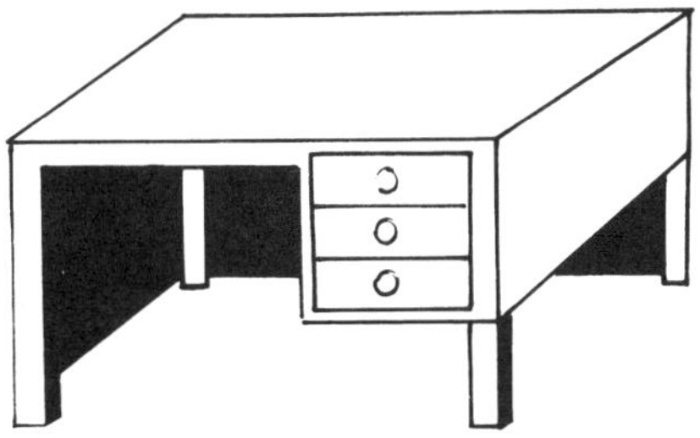 مَكْتَب

Malik  مَلِك

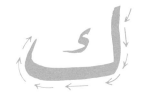

كَعْبَة مَكْتَب مَلِك

كَعْبَة مَكْتَب مَلِك

كَعْبَة مَكْتَب مَلِك

Qāf

ق قاف ق

Qur'ān  قُرآن

'Iqd  عِقُد

Ibrīq  إبرِيق

إبرِيق عِقُد قُرآن

إبرِيق عِقُد قُرآن

إبرِيق عِقُد قُرآن

Fā

ف فاء ف

فَم 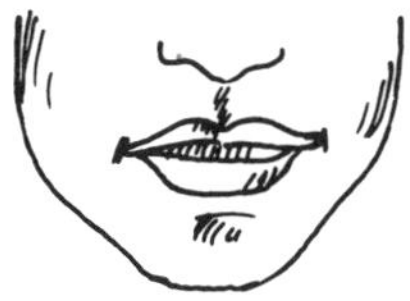 **Famm**

قَفَص  **Qafaṣ**

أَنْف  **Anf**

فَم قَفَص أَنْف

فَم قَفَص أَنف

فَم قَفَص أَنف

Ghain

غ غين غ

Ghurāb  غُرَاب

Baghl  بَغْل

Ṣamgh 

صَمْغ

غُرَاب بَغْل صَمْغ

غُرَاب بَغْل صَمْغ

غُرَاب بَغْل صَمْغ

‘Ain

ع عين ع

‘Inab  عِنَب

Sha‘r  شَعر

Jāmi‘  جَامِع

عِنَب شَعر جَامِع

عِنَب شَعر جَامِع

عِنَب شَعر جَامِع

Ẓā

ظ ظاء ظ

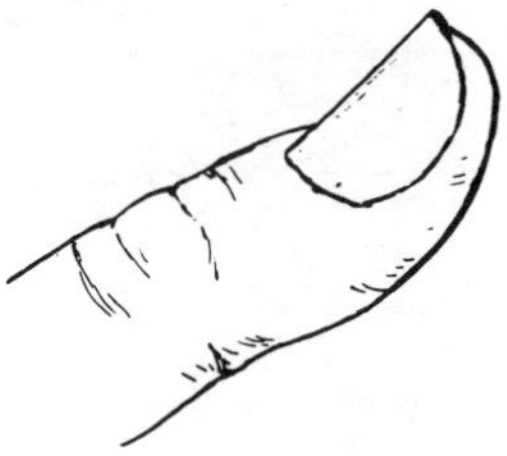

Ẓufr ظُفُر

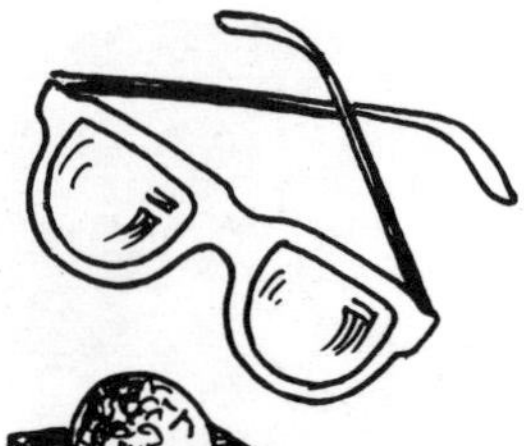

Naẓẓārah نَظَّارَة

Wā'iẓ وَاعِظ

وَاعِظ نَظَّارَة ظُفُر

وَاعِظ نَظَّارَة ظُفُر

وَاعِظ نَظَّارَة ظُفُر

Ṭā

ط طاء ط

Ṭair — طَيْر

Qiṭār — قِطَار

Khaiṭ — خَيْط

طَيْر قِطَار خَيْط

Dād

ض ضاد ض

Difdi‘  ضِفْدِع

Qadib  قَضِيْب

Baid  بَيْض

ضِفْدِع قَضِيْب بَيْض

ضِفْدِع قَضِيْب بَيْض

ضِفْدِع قَضِيْب بَيْض

Ṣād

ص صاد ص

Ṣūṣ  صُوص

Baṣal  بَصَل

Miqaṣ  مِقَصّ

مِقَصّ بَصَل صُوص

مِقَصّ بَصَل صُوص

مِقَصّ بَصَل صُوص

Shīn

ش شين ش

Shams  شَمْس

Minshār 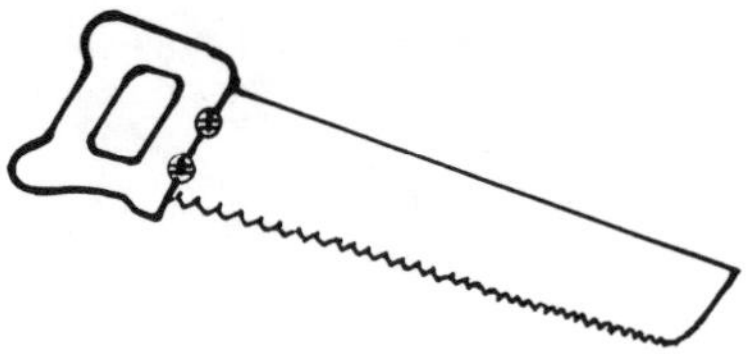 مِنْشَار

Rafsh  رَفْش

رَفْش	مِنْشَار	شَمْس
رَفْش	مِنْشَار	شَمْس
رَفْش	مِنْشَار	شَمْس

Sīn

س سين س

Samak سَمَكَة

Lisān لِسَان

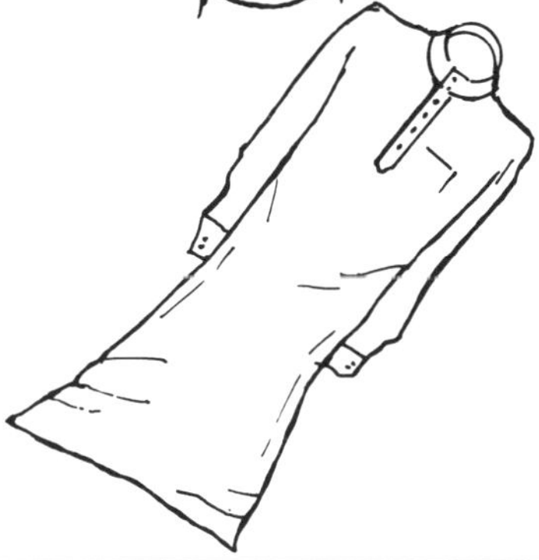

Libs لِبُس

سَمَكَة لِسَان لِبُس

سَمَكَة لِسَان لِبُس

سَمَكَة لِسَان لِبُس

Zā

ز زاء ز

Zahrah زَهُرَة

Mīzān مِيزَان

'Anz عَنُز

عَنُز	مِيزَان	زَهُرَة
عَنُز	مِيزَان	زَهُرَة
عَنُز	مِيزَان	زَهُرَة

Rā

ر راء ر

Rajul  رَجُل

Burtuqāl  بُرتُقَال

Qamar  قَمَر

رَجُل بُرتُقَال قَمَر

رَجُل بُرتُقَال قَمَر

رَجُل بُرتُقَال قَمَر

Dhāl

ذ ذال ذ

Dhurah 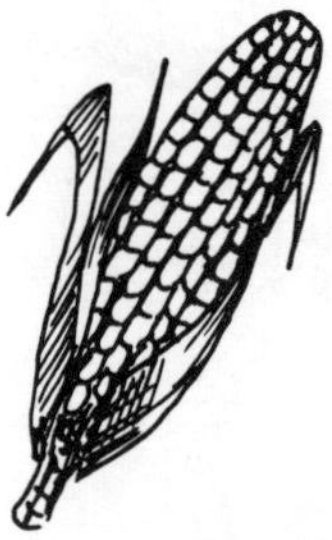 ذُرَة

Ḥidhā’  حِذَاء

Juradh  جُرَذ

جُرَذ	حِذَاء	ذُرَة
جُرَذ	حِذَاء	ذُرَة
جُرَذ	حِذَاء	ذُرَة

Dāl

د دال د

Dik دِيك

Hud Hud هُدهُد

'Iqd عِقْد

دِيك هُدهُد عِقْد

دِيك هُدهُد عِقْد

دِيك هُدهُد عِقْد

Khā

خ خاء خ

Kharūf خَرُوف

Nakhlah نَخْلَة

Baṭṭīkh بَطِّيخ

خَرُوف نَخْلَة بَطِّيخ

خَرُوف نَخْلَة بَطِّيخ

خَرُوف نَخْلَة بَطِّيخ

Ḥā

ح حاء ح

Ḥiṣān — حِصَان

Ṣaḥn — صَحُن

Rumḥ — رُمُح

حِصَان صَحُن رُمُح

حِصَان صَحُن رُمُح

حِصَان صَحُن رُمُح

Jīm

ج جيم ج

Jamal جَمَل

Shajarah شَجَرَة

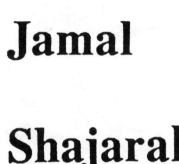

Thalj ثَلْج

ثَلْج شَجَرَة جَمَل

ثَلْج شَجَرَة جَمَل

ثَلْج شَجَرَة جَمَل

Thā

ث ثاء ث

Tha'lab  ثَعْلَب

Muthallath  مُثَلَّث

Laith  لَيْث

ثَعْلَب مُثَلَّث لَيْث

Tā

ت تاء ت

Tuffāḥ  تُفَّاح

Kitāb  كِتَاب

Takht 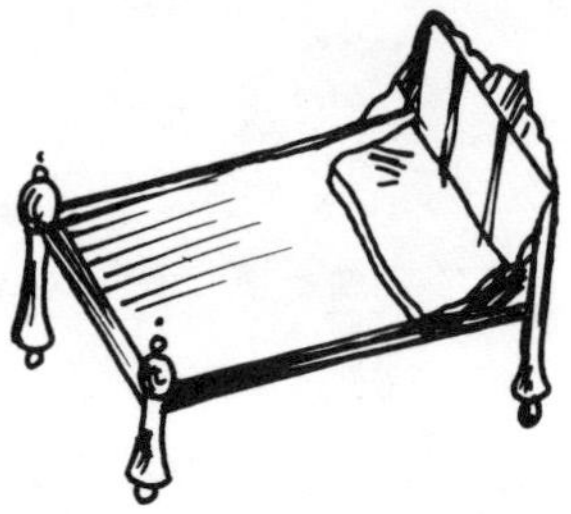 تَخْت

تُفَّاح كِتَاب تَخْت

تُفَّاح كِتَاب تَخْت

تُفَّاح كِتَاب تَخْت

Bā

ب (بـاء) ب

Baqarah — بَقَرَة

Jabal — جَبَل

'Inab — عِنَب

عِنَب	جَبَل	بَقَرَة
عِنَب	جَبَل	بَقَرَة
عِنَب	جَبَل	بَقَرَة

Alif

ا الف ا

Arnab  أَرْنَب

Sā‘ah  سَاعَة

Kūsā  كُوسَا

أَرْنَب	سَاعَة	كُوسَا
أَرْنَب	سَاعَة	كُوسَا
أَرْنَب	سَاعَة	كُوسَا

BEFORE WE START

This book is specially designed for children to teach them shape, form and inter-relationship of Arabic letters as part of a program of Arabic learning for the beginners.

There are total 28 Arabic letters. In writing they change their shape when written i) independent, ii) in the beginning, iii) in the middle and iv) as a final letter. Thus a student may have to learn to write not 28 but at least 109 letters. In most cases their change of form is not very different from original independent letter, that of course, makes it easy for the student to learn them. Learning to write Arabic is not as difficult as it appears and they will discover it soon.

Pay special attention to the following:

a) <u>Diacritical Marks</u>:
Some groups of Arabic letter are distinguished from each other through their <u>diacritical marks.</u>
For example look at:
bā = ب, tā = ت , thā = ث , nun = ن , yā = ي

They must remember their dots *(Nuqaṭ)* to find out which is which. Thus when they learn to write one letter they may learn two or more. All such groups must be clearly identified.

b) <u>Connector Letters</u>:
Most letters change their form when written in their independent, initial, medial and final form. See for example how (ع) changes shapes. Independent (ع); initial (عـ); medial (ـعـ); and final (ـع). You must pay special attention to these letters.

c) <u>Non-connector Letters</u>:
Some letters don't connect initially or medially and do not very much change finally. There should be no problem in learning these. These letters are: ا د ذ ر ز و

d) For <u>Sign of 'Sukun'</u> we are using here the sign of Sukun (') being consistent with Qur'ânic script instead of the more familiar sign (o).

Now the student should turn the page and see:

a) Each page has a special activity for the student to learn the four shapes of each letter i.e. i) independent letter, ii) initial letter, iii) medial letter, and iv) final letter.

b) Three words of Arabic objects familiar to them are selected to show how each letter is used in connection with other letters to write a word.

Now we want the student to:

1. Say the name of the letter aloud.
2. Color the independent letter and learn how to write it.
3. Say the Arabic names of the three objects on each page (meanings are given in the Glossary).
4. Color the letter only and learn its various forms.
5. Write the whole word.
6. Practicc writing the whole word.
7. Memorize the Arabic names of the object.

We hope by now the student has mastered *Sail Through with Arabic Letters* and *Up and Away with Arabic Numbers*. If so, they will find this book easy. If not, never mind, let them start. Practice makes a person perfect.

Assad Nimer Busool
American Islamic College
Chicago, U.S.A.

August 1989

بسم الله الرحمن الرحيم

TO NIMER AND LATIFAH

Introducing
IQRA' INTERNATIONAL EDUCATIONAL FOUNDATION

IQRA' International Educational Foundation (Chicago, Illinois, USA) has been established to respond to the growing need of Islamic education for our children, youth, and adults. The Foundation is a non-profit, non-political organization, incorporated in the state of Illinois.

Program of Islamic Studies: A Pilot Project

Subjects:
IQRA' has undertaken a pilot project, *A Comprehensive and Systematic Program of Islamic Studies* which includes seven subjects:

1. Arabic Studies.
2. The Qurānic Studies
3. *Sīrah* of *Rasulullah. Salla Allāhu 'Alaihi wa Sallam.*
4. *'Aqa'id* and *Fiqh.*
5. Islamic Social Studies (History, Geography ect.)
6. Islamic *Akhlāq.*
7. Islamic Education and Da'wah.
8. Islamic Literature.
9. English Language.

Educational Material:
The program comprises *graded textbooks, workbooks, parents/teachers manuals, enrichment literature, and educational aids.* The material is being prepared by experts in these areas of specialization.

Levels:
The Program incorporates three levels for children and youth -*Elementary, Junior, and Senior*- and two levels for adults, associates and bachelors.

Your Cooperation

The writing and production of quality Islamic educational material is a time consuming and expensive undertaking which requires the support of well -meaning Muslims committed to an Islamic future for themselves and for generations to come. Make a commitment by sending your contributions, publicizing IQRA' efforts and reading (and enjoying) IQRA' materials.

IQRA' BOOK CENTER

2749-51 Devon Ave.

Chicago Illinois, 60659

Phone: (773)-274-2665

Fax: (773)-274-8733

www.iqra.org

مسلسل: تسليـة مع الكتابـة العربيّـة   جزء ٢

أشكال الحُروف العَربيّة

TIRFIYA

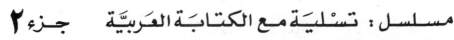

أسعد نمر بصول

مؤسسة إقرأ الثقافية العالمية
شيكاغو